HSING-I

Chinese Internal Boxing

HSING-I

Chinese
Internal Boxing

Robert W. Smith
and Allen Pittman

TUTTLE PUBLISHING
Boston • Rutland, Vermont • Tokyo

Published by Tuttle Publishing,
An imprint of Periplus Editions (HK) Ltd.

LCC Card No. 89-51716
ISBN 0-8048-1617-4

First edition, 1990
Eighth printing, 2001

Printed in Singapore

Distributed by:

Japan & Korea	*North America*	*Asia Pacific*
Tuttle Publishing	**Tuttle Publishing**	**Berkeley Books Pte. Ltd**
RK Building 2nd Floor	Distribution Center	130 Joo Seng Road
2-13-10 Shimo-Meguro, Meguro-ku	Airport Industrial Park	#06-01/03
Tokyo 153 0064	364 Innovation Drive	Olivine Building
Tel: (03) 5437 0171	North Clarendon, VT 05759-9436	Singapore 368357
Fax: (03) 5437 0755	Tel: (802) 773 8930	Tel: (65) 280 1330
	Fax: (802) 773 6993	Fax: (65) 280 6290

Contents

Preface

We wrote this book believing that there are many people who are interested in the Chinese internal martial art of Hsing-i (pronounced "shing-ee") as it was traditionally taught on the mainland.* Such people understand that this art is essentially a meditative form of health and body management from which self defense spills over, rather than an aggressive combat form, of which the world already has too many. As a system of self defense, however, it is harshly effective.

Besides training for several years in Taiwan under the Hsing-i masters Hung I-hsiang and his brother Hung I-mien, Mr. Smith was also fortunate enough to be allowed to study under Wang Shu-chin, Kuo Feng-ch'ih, Yuan Tao, and other masters. His training path is clearly outlined in his *Chinese Boxing: Masters and Methods* (Tokyo, 1974) and other books. Some twenty years later, Mr. Pittman, one of Mr. Smith's senior students, went to Taiwan seeking the old masters, but found that many had died. In Taipei, happily, he came across a still hardy Hung I-mien, who invited him to share his home as a live-in student. After absorbing Hung's Hsing-i and Pakua, he traveled south to Taichung to practice with the sons of Ch'en P'an-ling—Yuan-ch'ao and Yun-ch'ing—and the senior students of the late Wang Shu-chin.

From these experiences, the basic forms of these two master

*In this book, Chinese terms are transliterated with the Wade-Giles system, except where the word is already widely used with a different spelling, as, for instance, "Peking, "Nanking," etc.

1. Author Smith with Ch'en P'an-ling and Wang Shu-chin, 1962

teachers were assimilated and consolidated. This is first time that they have been taught to the West in such minute detail. We hope that Western students will benefit from this clear exposition of teachings that were once only passed on to initiates deemed worthy of learning the styles and being entrusted with their transmission.

The Hsing-i forms given in this book are essentially those of Ch'en P'an-ling (Fig. 1) as elaborated in his *Chung-hua kuo-shu chiao-ts'ai ch'uan-chi* [The Complete Instructional Guide to Chinese Martial Arts] (Taipei, 1978). These are the orthodox, traditional methods long practiced on the mainland and in Taiwan—the authentic forms from which most other versions derive. They are being published here so that students can learn the *real* forms as opposed to Americanized off-shoots. With them, you can refine your nature, reform your temperament, and return to your original self.

It is a rash reader who thinks that by simply buying this book he or she will absorb the teachings it contains. To learn any of the three internal arts—T'ai-chi, Hsing-i, or Pa-kua—requires commitment, not mere involvement. Being involved or committed is like ham and eggs: the chicken is involved but the pig is committed! This is not a coffee-table book—it should be sweat over and on. We have labored over its presentation, carefully blending the pictorial with the textual, so that the student can learn without going astray. But our efforts avail nothing if the student does not practice. He or she must practice assiduously for a long time—"The years see what the day will never know"—if progress is to come. Confucius once said that if he gave a student one corner of a handkerchief, it was up to the student to find the other three corners. This book is but one corner; your practice will help you find the other three.

Acknowledgments

The writing of this book was eased by the help and support of several friends and colleagues: John Lang, who diligently worked at every level of its preparation; James Klebau, a true professional, who caught the inner spirit of the forms in his fine photographs; Pat Kenny, who helped with the graphics; Bob Arief, Al Carson, Jay Falleson, Steve Goodson, and Irene Pittman, who proofread and corrected the manuscript; Y. W. Chang, Ann Carruthers, Pat McGowan, Chris Bates, Richard Cress, Danny Emerick, and Ben Lo, who acted as sounding-boards; Anne Pavay and Alice Smith, who patiently typed the manuscript; Stephen Comee, who studies under Wang Shu-chin's successor and who worked hard as the editor and designer of this book; the Charles E. Tuttle Company, which agreed to publish this book; and all the masters and teachers of the Chinese internal martial arts who have given their time and instruction—without their generosity we would never have been able to study these arts. To all of these and to others who helped bring this project to fruition, the authors gratefully bow in deep thanks.

Robert W. Smith
Allen Pittman

Flat Rock, NC

PART ONE	Introduction to Hsing-i Boxing

The theory of Hsing-i is simple. The aim is to divest ourselves of what we acquire after birth and return to the origin (the oneness) through the Five Fists and the Twelve Animal Styles. All of these derive from one style. Keeping the mind calm and at the tan-t'ien *(below the navel), we will come to the one.*

—*Master Liu Hsiao-lan*

1
What Is Hsing-i?

NAME AND THING

The name of this style of Chinese boxing, *hsing-i ch'uan,* literally means "the kind of boxing (*ch'uan*) in which the forms (*hsing*) are created by the mind (*i*)." In this "mind-formed fist," the mind predominates over mere physicality and, harmoniously blending thought and action, expresses itself in moving forms and postures dating back some 400 years.

Hsing-i is one of the three traditional Chinese forms of internal boxing, the other two being T'ai-chi ("tie-jee") and Pa-kua ("bahgwah").[1] Each of the three internal arts is a distinct style of boxing, yet each shares with the others the fact that it is essentially a form of moving meditation. Boxing is something of a misnomer. Each of the internal arts is actually a self-contained and complete system of exercise that is permeated with functions combining grappling and striking, and that, through correct practice, is seen to be a superior system of self-defense. Each of them, through diligent practice, becomes a part of your life. Self-improvement on all levels—physical, emotional, men-

---

[1] These internal fighting systems differ from the Shaolin and other external traditions in that they depend upon the practitioner's ability to cultivate and use *ch'i* rather than only outer muscular strength. Internal masters develop and use the sinews, ligaments, and tendons, whereas external masters concentrate on the larger outer musculature.

tal, and spiritual—is the reason we train in an art: it is there if needed, but it is used only in the greatest extremity because of its inherent power. In a utilitarian society, this might seem a silly motivation—to learn something so that you will never have to use it. But Hsing-i is an internal art, and, as such, it is more concerned with life, health, and creativity than with death, competition, or destruction.

Indeed, none of the internal arts has free sparring, which is a type of competitive fighting and which is avoided in learning the internal arts. Rather, we box mainly with ourselves, and by learning the skill there is no need to contest it. George Mallory, who died on Mount Everest in 1924, once explained why men climbed mountains (''Because they are there'') by asking, ''Whom have we conquered?'' and answering, ''None but ourselves.'' Internal boxing is essentially a method of transforming the self. The traditional Doctrine of Three Layers (*San-ts'eng t'ao-li*) discusses this process of change in terms of Taoist philosophy, wherein it is thought that one's original state (*hsu*, or emptiness) is filled by a seed-essence (*ching*) at birth, and that this life essence is so transformed into intrinsic energy (*ch'i*) and further into vital spirit (*shen*) through practice that one returns to the original state of emptiness (*hsu*). It advises the student to change essence into *ch'i*, *ch'i* into spirit, and then to restore to spirit the original emptiness. Put simply, the boxing is at once the tool and the product of this creative process. Because it is creative, it cannot lead to destruction. True enough, the old masters met challenges. But more often than not they sent the challenger away a friend—happy because he had been soundly defeated, educated but not seriously hurt.

The most famous such match reportedly occurred in Peking between Kuo Yun-shen, the famed Hsing-i adept known as ''the Divine Crushing Fist,'' and Tung Hai-ch'uan, the modern father of Pa-kua. Kuo tried unsuccessfully for two days to dent Tung's defense and on the third day was completely defeated by the Pa-kua master. The two

2. The "Crushing Fist" of Hsing-i, Peking, ca. 1930

became lifelong friends; indeed, so impressed were they with the art of the other that they signed a pact requiring students of each discipline to cross-train in the other. Thus, to this day, the systems are coupled, complementary, and taught together. In fact, the principles cited for Hsing-i in this book are equally applicable to Pa-kua.

Done correctly, Hsing-i strikes are extremely dangerous. That is why there is no sparring: if the punches are pulled or muted in any way, they are not Hsing-i. Thus, Western boxing and karate cannot help the Hsing-i boxer to sharpen his skills. In this respect, Hsing-i is similar to the ancient forms of some Japanese martial arts, which have remained the same over the centuries because of their difficulty and intrinsically dangerous natures. If regulated, restricted, and made sportive, such arts, including Hsing-i and Pa-kua, lose their essence.

Hsing-i nonetheless proved its worth in regulated Chinese national boxing tournaments: its exponents led the winners of the tournaments held in Nanking (1928), Shanghai (1929), Hangchou (1929), and again in Nanking (1933). The most successful provincial competitions were conducted in Honan province by Ch'en P'an-ling, whose method we teach here.

Being a form of meditation, Hsing-i requires strong dedication to regular practice in a quiet place (Fig. 2). You must create for yourself

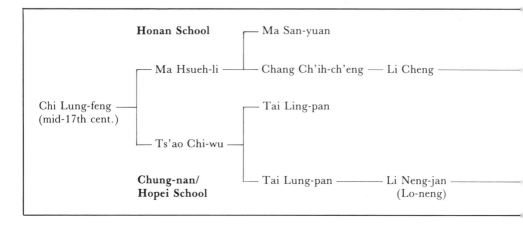

Table 1. Abbreviated Hsing-i Lineage

a routine based on a quiet attentiveness, which may at first bore you. Ultimate skill comes from this quiet as much as from the physiological and psychological aspects of the exercise itself. When the silence releases its energy, a quiet mind is produced and your whole being becomes more active.

A system relying totally on body mechanics remains at the level of calisthenics and rudimentary fighting, Hsing-i trains the mind even more than it does the body. The mind *wills* and the body *responds*. There is a kind of reciprocity at work, for as the body is exercised dynamically and internally it returns health benefits to both itself and the mind. And the process continues, the mind being the master.

Springing from Taoist and Buddhist techniques, Hsing-i is cooperative, not competitive; it emphasizes *being* and *becoming* rather than *thinking* and *doing*. But it requires discipline and much hard work. Because Hsing-i gets little media reinforcement, you must motivate and sustain yourself. Progress will be slower than in the external arts, but since the skill you achieve comes from your mind and your internal organs, it will be deeper and will last longer.

---

[1] Conservative (orthodox) school

[2] Natural school

[3] Comprehensive school; Sun is also thought to have studied directly under both Kuo Yun-shen and Li Ts'un-i.

[4] Wang was the first teacher to bring T'ai-chi to Japan (1958); the training hall he opened in Tokyo's Shibuya district still teaches T'ai-chi, Hsing-i, and Pa-kua as taught by Wang.

HISTORY AND MASTERS

Traditionally, it is taught that Hsing-i was created by a general of the Northern Sung dynasty (960–1127) named Yueh Fei; and some even credit its genesis to Bodhidharma, the monk who brought Zen from India to China in the sixth century—neither of these claims can be substantiated. Both are the stuff of legend.

What is known with certainty is that a man named Chi Lung-feng is the earliest recorded father of the art, but we know very little about him save that he was from Shanghai, excelled in spear-play, and learned Hsing-i in the Chung-nan mountains of Shansi province between 1637 and 1662 from a Taoist hermit. Chi's top two students, Ts'ao

Chi-wu of Shansi and Ma Hsueh-li of Honan, spread the art to others through whom the teachings have come down to the present in two lines of unbroken succession. Honan, Hopei, and Shansi supplied most of the great teachers, among whom were: Li Neng-jan, Sung Shih-jung, Chang Chih-ch'eng, Ch'e I-chai, Kuo Yun-shen, Li Cheng, Li Ts'un-i, Shang Yun-hsiang, Wang Hsiang-chai, Sun Lu-t'ang, Ch'en P'an-ling, Chang Chun-feng, and Wang Shu-chin (Table 1). Ch'en P'an-ling studied the orthodox Hsing-i system taught in this book directly from the great Li Ts'un-i.

2
Theories Behind the Art

BREATHING AND BODY

Correct breathing uses the diaphragm, a large muscle that stretches from the lumbar spine to the rib cage, separating the heart-lung area from the digestive organs. Abdominal breathing articulates the intercostal muscles and ribs and efficiently positions the shoulder blades and clavicles, thus assisting coordination of the upper torso and supporting the head and arms. All movements are coordinated with the breathing, achieving, as master Sung Shih-jung wrote, "full calmness, full regulation of breathing, and full coordination of the body." Initially, breathe naturally without thinking of inhalation and exhalation. Breathe only through your nostrils, filling your belly. Keep your tongue on the roof of your mouth, your lips relaxed. Later, pay attention to your inhalation, sinking the *ch'i* (intrinsic energy) to your *tan-t'ien* (the psychic center just below the navel). Specifically, when practicing the forms, you should exhale through the nostrils as you apply the movement, but simultaneously, sink a part of the breath down to the *tan-t'ien*. If you reach the top level of the art, you will not be conscious of breathing. As master Kuo Yun-shen wrote: "There is no sound, no smell, and everything is empty."

Hsing-i enlivens your muscles by expansion and contraction, strengthens the ligaments and tendons, eases the circulation of both the blood and *ch'i,* and produces rapid, effortless movement. The muscles and sinews are made more elastic and lively while being strengthened in a process similar to that of the refining of raw iron into steel. Open your body: become familiar with the pull of gravity and with a precise, straight posture. Relax your shoulders: become aware of the position of the shoulder blades. Bend your legs: become aware of the way you hold the pelvis. Hold your neck straight: keep the head erect, as though it were being pulled up with a string, and look directly ahead. Relax your buttocks, holding the sacrum naturally straight.

These training principles bearing on the muscles are important, but if you pay attention only to the external musculature, the blood and *ch'i* will not be able to circulate freely—and *ch'i* is the foundation of the art. It must be sunk to the *tan-t'ien,* whence it circulates throughout the body. The ancients said that the original *ch'i* (*yuan ch'i*)—"the power that keeps the sky blue and the earth calm and also makes for achievement in man"—must be maintained. Besides cultivating your *ch'i,* you must also rid yourself of bad habits and thoughts, calm your heart, and thus attain sincerity.

Hsing-i gives good health and makes your body strong. Your internal organs are like the engine parts of a car, your muscles like its outer surface. Blood and *ch'i* are the fuel generating movement. If the engine parts are broken, the car will not run, even if it is full of gasoline and looks fine. Therefore, priority is given to the internal organs, which leads to a natural cultivation of *ch'i,* rather than to the outer muscles.

Coming from stillness, the upright postures teach grounding by lowering the waist and pelvis, relaxing the buttocks, and bending the legs. The rhythm of the movements provides aerobic benefits, while the alternate training of moving and pausing assists the sense of timing and rooting. *Natural* coordination is "restored" through movements stressing opposite-hand-and-foot substantiality as well as synchronized same-hand-and-foot movements. Finally, because balance is lost when you place your weight 50-50 between your legs ("double weighting"),

Hsing-i depends upon single-weighted, "one-legged" boxing that allows you to distinguish the empty (*yin*) and the full (*yang*) and that enhances freer movement.

EXERCISE AND MEDITATION

Like Pa-kua, Hsing-i derives from ancient Buddhist and especially Taoist meditation practices. The physiological and esoteric principles have been explicated by master Kuo Yun-shen, and what follows in this section is a summary of his teachings. Taoist meditation and internal boxing both have the goal of emptiness. But where meditation goes from inaction to action, boxing goes in the opposite direction, from action to inaction. From the Taoists, the Hsing-i masters borrowed the following concept of changes:

Hsing-i Stages	Taoist Sedentary Changes	Body Changes	Type of Energy
1. Change essence to *ch'i*	Hard burning	Bones	Visible
2. Change *ch'i* to spirit	Summoning fire	Sinews	Concealed
3. Change spirit to emptiness	Divine fire	Marrow	Mysterious

To get visible energy, you must be centered and balanced. This energy transforms essence (actually connoting but meaning much more than just sexual energy) into *ch'i*, which changes the bones. When you stand and move, your bones become hard and your body becomes solid like a mountain. After rigorous practice for an extended period, your dispersed *ch'i* is concentrated at your navel and all parts of your body become coordinated.

The next stage is concealed energy. Developing from the first stage, it is free, relaxed, and natural. It is not soft like snow, but elastic like grass. Here, *ch'i* is transformed into vital spirit and the sinews are energized.

In the next and highest stage, that of mysterious energy, the bone marrow is washed and cleaned, relaxation is complete, and your internal organs are so purified that you become as light as a feather. The energy becomes so concentrated that its nature is restored to that of original emptiness. Your actions are the same, but your energy remains inside, controlled by the mind.

But how does Hsing-i manifest itself in these three stages? Traditionally, it is described thus: in the visible stage, it is "like a steel chisel that thrusts out strongly and falls lightly like a piece of bamboo"; in the concealed stage, it "starts like an arrow and falls weightlessly, like the wind"; and in the highest stage, it "follows the wind and chases the moon." An outsider never sees it hit. Here, the mind is mindless; you do nothing and have done everything. In the emptiness you find your pre-birth energy, but if you search too hard it will elude you. It is better to think that you already possess such energy. This will influence your mind, the embodiment of all actions. Remember—Hsing-i is boxing with the mind.

PART TWO Hsing-i Training

3
The Basics

All Hsing-i movements are performed lightly and briskly, and the entire body is relaxed, without the strong muscular contraction of karate and other external forms. To learn to do Hsing-i properly, you must first master the following fundamentals.

THE FIVE POSITIONS

Chicken Leg	One leg supports the body while the other is held off the ground.
Dragon Body	The body stands in three straight sections: heels to knees, knees to hips, and hips to head.
Bear Shoulders	The shoulders are rounded, curving from the spine like a bow.
Eagle Claws	The fingers clutch tightly like talons.
Tiger Embrace	The arms menace threateningly, looking like a tiger leaving its den.

THE SIX COORDINATIONS

The six coordinations are extremely important to the correct practice of Hsing-i, since, if the *ch'i* and the movement are not coordinated, then the posture will be incorrect and you will not be able to use your *ch'i*. If the body is straight and does not lean in any direction, the mind will be clear, the *ch'i* will be harmonious, and the movement will be natural. Thus, internally, the spirit controls the mind, which controls the *ch'i*, which controls the strength. Externally, the hands pressing downward correlate with the heels turning outward; the sinking of the elbows is correlated with the slight inward pressing of the knees; and the shoulders and thighs relax. Total *true* movement can come about only if these six coordinations are unified, harmonized, and maintained.

Internal	External	
Spirit — Mind	Shoulders — Thighs	
Mind — *Ch'i*	Elbows	— Knees
Ch'i — Strength	Hands	— Feet

THE NINE WORDS

1) Press your head upward, your tongue forward and upward (so that it touches the upper palate), and your palms strongly to the front.

2) When you "button down" your shoulders, the chest empties and *ch'i* flows freely to the elbows. When you "button down" your hands and feet, the palms and soles empty and *ch'i* flows freely to them. When your teeth "button down," your tendons and bones contract.

3) By rounding your back, your strength "urges" the body, your coccyx straightens, and your spirit rises. By rounding the chest, the elbows protect the heart and the breath (*ch'i*) moves freely. By rounding the tiger's mouth (*hu k'ou*, the space be-

tween the thumb and index finger), your energy (*ching*) is directed outward and your arms develop "embracing" energy.

4) Learn to keep your mind (heart: *hsin*) relaxed so that it can respond to any situation, to keep your eyes alert, and to keep your hands ahead of your enemy (i.e., to move them in such a way that the enemy cannot see them strike).

5) Hold your *ch'i* securely within your *tan-t'ien*; hold your upper breath gently so that fear has no place in which to take hold; and hold your ribs safely within the elbows, so that there is no way for danger to approach them.

6) When you sink your *ch'i* down into your *tan-t'ien*, you will become as stable as a mountain. When you sink your shoulders, your arms will spring to life, "urged" on by the elbows. When you sink your arms, they naturally protect the ribs.

7) When you bend your arms, strength will be abundant. When you bend your knees, you will be rooted to the earth with strength. When you cup your palms, strength will concentrate in them. When you bend or curve these parts of the body, they naturally contract and expand, thus unblocking the flow of energy.

8) When you straighten your neck, your head will become erect, as though floating in the air, and your *ch'i* will rise up strongly. When you straighten your spine, your strength will reach the four extremities (the top of the head, the hands, the knees, and the feet) and *ch'i* will fill the whole body. When you straighten your knees, the flow of your *ch'i* will be calm and your spirit will be harmonious, making you like a tree sending roots down deep into the earth, from which it absorbs energy.

9) Hold you arms so that they embrace the chest, protecting your

3–7. The Basic Motions: 3) Starting Position; 4) Rise; 5) Drill;

heart and ready to strike out like a tiger lunging at its prey. Keep your *ch'i* down so that it embraces the *tan-t'ien*, allowing the *ch'i* to flow freely throughout the body. Let your courage rise up and embrace the body; this will let your *ch'i* flow so freely that it covers the body with a mantle of protection.

OTHER POINTERS

Some other pointers that should be kept in mind when practicing are:
1) The tip of your nose, your fingertips, and the tips of your toes should be kept on one imaginary line.
2) Your body should fall as your *ch'i* rises, and should rise as your *ch'i* falls.
3) Your hands should rise like iron spades and fall like scythes.
4) When you use but one hand, it should thrust out like a hawk raiding a forest and fall like a swallow sweeping over the surface of a lake. When you use both hands, they should rise up like a tiger leaping out of its lair and fall like a sledgehammer breaking bricks.
5) The fundamental tactic—and one that the old masters practiced by the hour—is the same as in Pa-kua: rise, drill, fall, and overturn (Figs. 3–7). Each part must be clearly differentiated; all must be done like lightning. This is eased by keeping your body relaxed until the final instant. The tactic can be

6) Fall; and 7) Overturn

used—either quickly or slowly—in all directions to close up the distance between you and your opponent.

6) Summarizing, your

waist — sinks
shoulders — shrink
chest — withdraws
head — pushes up
tongue — touches the roof of the mouth
hands — feel as if pushing upward
sacrum — circles inward and upward

4

Practicing the Five Fists

H sing-i's five basic forms are also called the five elements (*wu hsing*), after the five essential elements of traditional Chinese cosmology—metal, water, wood, fire, and earth. Each of these elements is capable of generating or destroying another element, as shown in the diagram below. The lines forming the pentagon indicate generation, while those forming the star indicate destruction.

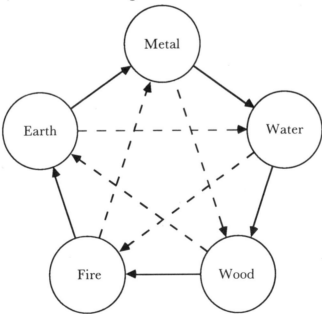

The FIVE FISTS were originally arranged in the same sequence as the order of generation of elements from metal to earth, and some schools of the orthodox Chung-nan line, such as Wang Shu-chin's, still follow that order, each fist symbolizing an element that generates the next one. Sun Lu-t'ang, Yuan Tao, Chen P'an-ling, and others in the orthodox school, however, reversed the order of water and wood, placing CRUSHING before DRILLING (Table 2). Thus, that is the sequence we have presented here.

The FIVE FISTS are as natural as a baby's movements. But because they are natural, they are difficult for people in a tense world to learn, and, after long practice, they can be dangerous if not controlled. They are correlated with the five elements, the organs of the body, and the flow of *ch'i* as follows:

Table 2.   The Five Correspondences

Fist	Element	Organs	Action of *Ch'i*
1. SPLITTING (*p'i-ch'uan*)	Metal	Lungs, Large Intestine	Rises and falls like an axe
2. CRUSHING (*peng-ch'uan*)	Wood	Liver, Gall bladder	Expands and contracts simultaneously
3. DRILLING (*tsuan-ch'uan*)	Water	Kidneys, Bladder	Flows in curving eddies or shoots like lightning
4. POUNDING (*p'ao-ch'uan*)	Fire	Heart, Pericardium	Fires suddenly like a projectile from a gun
5. CROSSING (*heng-ch'uan*)	Earth	Spleen, Stomach	Strikes forward with rounded energy

8

PREPARATION

The static INFINITY POSTURE (*wu chi*), a balance between suspension and rootedness, is the basis for Hsing-i movement. Your feet are at 45°, left foot facing front and heels touching, with the legs straight but with the knees slightly bent, and the pelvis is held in a natural position. Your head is suspended, allowing your spine to straighten. Relaxed shoulders that hang naturally in line with your hips allow the weight of your upper body to fall directly over your pelvic girdle and into your legs, creating the sense of "suspended by the crown of the head and rooted in the feet." Your mind and *ch'i* are centered in the *tan-t'ien* (Fig. 8).

9   10   11

BEGINNING

Stand in the INFINITY POSTURE and raise both arms out to the sides, palms down, twisting your torso slightly rightward (Fig. 9). Take your hands past your shoulders overhead, shoulder width apart, palms still down (Fig. 10). Continuing with your torso turned to the right, keep your knees together and sink your body as you lower your palms down the front of your body and close them into fists, while shifting most of your weight onto your right foot (Fig. 11).

Turn your waist leftward, DRILLING your right fist upward and forward (Fig. 12), palm up, to eyebrow level. Simultaneously, withdraw your left fist, palm down, to your left hip (Fig. 13). As you step forward with your left foot, DRILL your left fist upward (Fig. 14), open it, and strike with it over your retreating right fist, which open palm down near your groin. Your left foot is now on a line slightly to the left (about a fist's width) of your right heel (Fig. 15). The length of your advancing step should accord with your height.

You are now in the *san-t'i* ("three essentials") posture, the basic Hsing-i posture, which generates both the FIVE FISTS and the TWELVE ANIMALS (Fig. 16). Your head should press up as if balancing a book, your elbows and shoulders should be held down, and your knees should be well bent, thus lowering your hips, forming a crease where your lower abdomen and thighs meet (the inguinal area). Your weight should be distributed so that the rear leg supports 60% of it. Your left arm should be extended, the elbow slightly bent and the fingertips at eyebrow level. Your left hand should be open and stretched to form the

12   13   14

INCORRECT

CORRECT

15. The Width of the Advancing Step in Hsing-i

16

"tiger mouth" as it strikes forward. Your open right hand should be held palm down, but the fingers pointed upward to protect the groin. Finally, your eyes look at your left index finger, gazing past it, focusing on a point ahead.

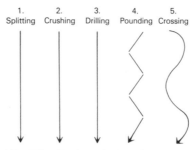

1.　　2.　　3.　　4.　　5.
Splitting　Crushing　Drilling　Pounding　Crossing

17. The Paths of the Five Fists

18　　19　　20

THE FIVE FISTS

1. SPLITTING FIST (*P'i ch'uan*)

The SPLITTING FIST moves directly ahead (Fig. 17). Continuing from *san-t'i,* as you shift your weight rearward, retract both of your hands into fists downward as if pulling on a rope (Fig. 18). Take a small step forward with your left foot, toed out at 45° and DRILL forward with both fists as you shift your weight onto your left foot. Your left fist leads your right fist, DRILLING, and ends, palm up, at eyebrow level. Your right fist touches your left forearm between the wrist and the elbow (Fig. 19).

Next, suspend your right foot at your left ankle (Fig. 20). Then take a full step forward with your right foot, pushing off your left foot. (Kuo

21   22   23

24   25

Yun-shen said: "The rear foot holds strength as though you are going to leap off it across a ditch"; but step, don't jump.) Open your fists, palms down, SPLITTING your right hand over your retracting left, as all your weight shifts forward onto your right foot (Fig. 21). Next, follow-step a half-step forward with your left foot and shift 60% of your weight back to it (Fig. 22).

> NOTE: All striking steps push off the rear foot and follow-
> steps are always half-steps.

Repeat the posture on the other side by reversing the above directions. From the right *san-t'i* position, pull back and down with both hands (Fig. 23), DRILL both fists forward as you shift your weight forward to your toed-out right foot (Fig. 24), suspend your left foot at your right ankle (Fig. 25), and step forward with your left foot as you SPLIT for-

26 27 28

29 30

ward with your left palm, accompanied by your right palm in a two-handed chop (Fig. 26). Pull backward with your waist and two hands (Fig. 27), take a left toed-out step while screwing your palm-up fists forward, the left leading (Fig. 28). Then, suspending your right foot at your left ankle (Fig. 29), take it forward, accompanied by your right hand, while your left hand drops to protect your groin (Fig. 30).

To turn back, shift your weight to your left foot; then toe in your right foot and shift your weight to it while dropping your fists to your

31 32

33 34

hips (Fig. 31). Then take a half-step forward with your left foot, toed out, DRILL your fists forward, suspend your right foot at your left ankle and then take it a full step forward while SPLITTING with both palms forward (Figs. 32–34). After striking, shift 60% of your weight back to your left foot. Continue as before, and after two more repetitions, when your right foot and palm are ahead, you may turn around again. (Three postures in one direction are conventional, but five, seven, or more can be done if there is room.)

35   36   37

38   39

2. CRUSHING FIST *(Peng ch'uan)*

The CRUSHING FIST moves directly ahead (Fig. 17). From a left *san-t'i* (Fig. 35), begin to pull your left hand back to your left hip, clenching it into a palm-up fist. Simultaneously, begin to extend your right hand, clenching it into a vertical fist.

Take a short step directly forward with your left foot (Fig. 36), shift most of your weight to it, and CRUSH with your right fist directly ahead. Pay attention to retracting your left hand, thus augmenting the power of your right punch. Follow-step with your right foot and shift 60% of your weight back to it. Sit into the posture and maintain the inguinal fold (Fig. 37).

To alternate sides, take a half-step forward with your left foot, toed out 45° (Figs. 38, 39), suspend your right foot at your left ankle,

40   41   42

43   44   45

pause, and then take it forward (Figs. 40, 41). Simultaneously, retract your right fist, palm up, and CRUSH forward with your left fist (Fig. 42). After follow-stepping with your left foot, shift 60% of your weight back to it.

To turn back, shift most of your weight back to your left foot, toe-in your right foot, and bring your fists, palms down, to your hips (Fig. 43). Shift your weight to your right foot and take a half-step with your left foot, CRUSH ahead with your right fist while retracting your left fist, and follow-step with your right foot, shifting 60% of your weight back to it (Figs. 44, 45). Continue as before, doing another posture, so that your right foot and left fist are ahead before turning again. The number of repetitions is governed by space. In the CRUSHING fist, you must do any even number of repetitions before turning around.

46

47

48

3. DRILLING FIST *(Tsuan ch'uan)*

The DRILLING FIST moves directly ahead (Fig. 17). From a left *san-t'i* (Fig. 46), toe-out your left foot and shift all your weight to it while you raise your left palm high and circle inward. The palm should be held straight ahead of you, at eyebrow level, palm out, with fingers pointing to the right, as though depressing an opponent's strike. At the same time, retract your right hand, palm up, to your right hip and suspend your right foot at your left ankle (Fig. 47). There should be some tension of "pulling apart" between your left palm and your right fist.

Pushing off your left foot, step forward with your right foot and DRILL your right fist over your depressing left palm. Stop your right fist at eyebrow level and move your left palm, changed to a palm-down

49

50

fist, beneath your right elbow. Follow-step with your left foot and shift 60% of your weight back to it (Fig. 48).

To alternate sides, reverse the directions given above. Circle your right hand up to eyebrow level while taking a half-step forward with your toed-out right foot, suspending your left foot at your right ankle, and simultaneously retracting your palm-up left fist to your left hip (Fig. 49). After a brief pause, push off with your right foot, step forward with your left foot, and DRILL with your left fist, palm up, over your depressing right palm, which changes to a palm-down fist, beneath your left elbow (Fig. 50).

Next, take a half-step with your left foot forward while circling your left hand to eyebrow level, suspend your right foot at your left ankle,

51   52

and retract your palm-up right fist to your right hip (Fig. 51). Then
step forward with your right foot, DRILLING your right fist to eyebrow
level and moving your left palm, changed to a palm-down fist, beneath
your right elbow. Follow-step with your left foot and shift 60% of your
weight back to it (Fig. 52).

To turn back with your right fist ahead, simply toe-in your right
foot and bring your palm-down right fist to your right hip. Step out
with your toed-out left foot, circle your left palm up as before, and
turn your right fist palm up at your right hip. At the same time, suspend your right foot at your left ankle briefly and take it forward while
DRILLING your right fist, palm up, over your depressing left palm,
which moves as a palm-down fist beneath your right elbow. Follow-
step with your left foot and shift 60% of your weight back to it. Then,
continue as before, doing two more repetitions before your right foot
and palm are ahead and you can turn around again. Three postures
are usually done here, but if there is room you can continue for five,
seven, or any odd number of repetitions. The turning movements are
identical with those described above.

53   54

55   56

4. POUNDING FIST   *(P'ao ch'uan)*

The POUNDING FIST moves forward in a zig-zag fashion (Fig. 17).
From a left *san-t'i* (Fig. 53), sink your weight into your right foot as
you pull both hands down in palm-up fists to near your right hip,
simultaneously suspending your left foot at your right ankle (Fig. 54).

Step with your left foot toward the left diagonal, pushing off your
right foot while raising your left fist, palm in, and prepare to POUND
with your vertical right fist (Fig. 55). As your weight shifts onto your
left foot, turn your left forearm outward, deflecting an upper strike
from an opponent, and POUND diagonally toward the left with your
right vertical fist slightly lower than your shoulder (Fig. 56). Follow-
step with the right foot as before, and shift 60% of your weight to it.

Alternate sides by shifting more weight to your right foot and taking

THE FIVE FISTS · **45**

57

58

59

60

a half-step toward the diagonal with your left foot (Fig. 57). Chamber your fists, palm up, near your left side, and suspend your right foot at your left ankle (Fig. 58). Then take a full step toward the right diagonal with your right foot, raising your right fist, palm up (Fig. 59). Now, as your weight shifts onto your right foot and your right arm rotates upward in deflecting, POUND with your left vertical fist. Then follow-step with your left foot as before (Fig. 60).

To turn around, pivot on your heels, toeing-in your right foot and turning your left foot outward. Shift your weight fully to your left foot, chamber your fists to your left hip, and suspend your right foot at your left ankle. Now proceed as before, stepping with your right foot to the right diagonal while deflecting with your right arm and POUND with your left vertical fist. If space permits, you may do four, six, or any even number of repetitions before your next turn.

61   62

63   64

5. CROSSING FIST (*Heng ch'uan*)

The CROSSING FIST moves forward in a wavy fashion (Fig. 17). From a left *san-t'i* (Fig. 61), step forward diagonally to the left with your left foot, pushing off your right foot (Fig. 62). As your left foot is put down with the toes pointing directly ahead, close your right hand into a fist and start swinging it across your body clockwise, passing your navel, palm down, while your left hand closes into a fist in front of you (Fig. 63).

As you shift more of your weight to your left foot, continue CROSSING your right arm out from under your left until your right fist is palm up. Simultaneously, withdraw your left fist, palm down, to a point near your navel. Follow-step with your right foot as before (Fig. 64).

65   66   67

68   69

To alternate sides, take a half-step diagonally to the left, placing your left foot down with the toes pointing straight ahead (Fig. 65) and suspend your right foot at your left ankle (Fig. 66). Next, move your right foot diagonally to the right, toes pointing straight ahead (Fig. 67), CROSSING your left fist counterclockwise, underneath and around the retracting right fist (Fig. 68) and out to eyebrow level. Your left fist ends palm up; your right fist, palm down (Fig. 69). Follow-step with your left foot as before.

To turn back, shift your weight to the left and toe-in your right foot. Now take a half-step ahead with your left foot and CROSS your right fist from under your retracting left fist, and follow-step with your right foot as before. Continue doing the CROSSING fist for as many repetitions as you like, turning back only when your right foot is forward. Thus, two, four, or any even number of repetitions may be done.

70

71

72

ENDING

By substituting the DRAGON STYLE for the turning maneuver for any of the FIVE FISTS, you can close and end that series. This is done by toeing-in your right foot and raising your right hand, opening it palm down at eyebrow level. Your left hand opens near your right elbow (Fig. 70). Toe-out your left foot, pivoting on your heel, and turn your torso leftward (Fig. 71). Bend your knees, transferring most of your weight to your left foot, and raise your right heel off the ground.

Simultaneously, press (SPLIT) forward with your right palm, fingers at eyebrow level, while your left palm follows your right elbow (Fig. 72). Next, toe-in your left foot slightly, put your right heel beside your

73   74

75   76

left and lower your hands, palms facing the *tan-t'ien* (Fig. 73). Inhale and raise your arms out to the sides and upward as you twist your body rightward (Fig. 74). Press your palms down the center of your body and bend your knees together as you exhale (Fig. 75). Stand up in the INFINITY POSTURE (Fig. 76).

30′   31′

LINKING THE FIVE FISTS

After practicing the FIVE FISTS independently, moving back and forth in a straight line, you may link them sequentially as you turn after each series. A standard integrated set might look like this:

1) SPLITTING FIST: 3 repetitions, turning into
2) CRUSHING FIST: 4 repetitions, turning into
3) DRILLING FIST: 3 repetitions, turning into
4) POUNDING FIST: 4 repetitions, turning into
5) CROSSING FIST: 4 repetitions, turning into
   DRAGON STYLE and INFINITY POSTURE, which
   close the entire set.

Only two repetitions are shown for the CRUSHING, POUNDING, and CROSSING FISTS, but the fact that the extra two repetitions are identical with the first two obviate the need to illustrate them. Note also that the DRAGON STYLE is done in the integrated form only after the CROSSING FIST, closing the entire set. Instead, you simply merge one FIST with the next after you turn.

For example, on the third step of the SPLITTING FIST, with your right hand and right foot forward (Fig. 30′), swing back leftward as

44'   45'   37'

47'   52'

31'   58'   59'

60′

56′

described above (Fig. 31′), take a short step with your left foot, and then do a CRUSHING FIST (Figs. 44′, 45′).

To change the CRUSHING FIST into the DRILLING FIST, when your right foot and left fist are forward (Fig. 37′), swing leftward, taking a short step ahead with the left foot and shifting your weight forward on-to it; then suspend your right foot at your left ankle as you extend your left arm out ahead of your eyebrows (Fig. 47′).

To change the DRILLING FIST into the POUNDING FIST, when your right hand and right foot are forward (Fig. 52′), turn back leftward (Fig. 31′). Retract your left foot to your right ankle as you pull back with both hands (Fig. 58′) and then step ahead diagonally to the left as your hands deflect, striking in the POUNDING FIST (Figs. 59′, 60′).

Ending in the POUNDING FIST with your right foot and left fist for-ward (Fig. 56′), change into the CROSSING FIST by turning around

THE FIVE FISTS · **53**

63'

64'

69'

70'

71'

72′ 73′ 74′

75′

76′

leftward as before, then move your left foot diagonally across to the left and swing your right fist clockwise under your left elbow, doing the CROSSING FIST (Figs. 63′, 64′).

Finally, to close the CROSSING FIST sequence and the entire set, when your left fist and right foot are forward (Fig. 69′), turn around leftward into the DRAGON STYLE as described above (Figs. 70′–75′) and end in the INFINITY POSTURE (Fig. 76′).

THE FIVE FISTS · 55

5

Practicing the Twelve Animal Styles

Because of his intelligence, man is superior to other animals. Physically, however, he is unable to match the fighting ability of most animals. To the fundamental FIVE FISTS, therefore, Hsing-i adds twelve styles derived from the fighting characteristics of twelve animals, some mythical. Quite aside from their combatant functions, these styles exercise all parts of the body vigorously, and, with the mind leading and the *ch'i* sunk to the *tan-t'ien,* make a rigorous training regimen.

The names, types, and arrangement of the TWELVE ANIMAL STYLES vary according to the different schools of Hsing-i. The order in which Ch'en P'an-ling taught them is as follows:

1) dragon;	7) falcon;
2) tiger;	8) swallow;
3) monkey;	9) snake;
4) horse;	10) *t'ai* (a mythical bird);
5) water strider;	11, 12) combined eagle and bear.
6) cock;	

BEGINNING

As in the FIVE FISTS, face diagonally to the right, your heels touching and feet held 45° apart, the left foot pointing straight ahead (Fig. 77).

77 78 79 80

Raise your hands laterally, reaching above your head and gradually turn your palms down while turning your waist slightly rightward (Fig. 78). Press your arms down the front of your body, clenching your fists, palms down, at your navel, as you lower your body by bending your knees (Fig. 79). While shifting most of your weight onto your right foot, turn your waist leftward, DRILLING your right fist upward and forward, palm up, to eyebrow level (Fig. 80). Simultaneously, retract your left fist, palm down, to your left hip. Now, as you step forward with your left foot such that the heels of your feet are on parallel lines about a fist's width apart, DRILL your left fist upward, open it, and SPLIT with it over your retracting right fist, which opens, palm down, near your groin. You are now in *san-t'i*, the basic starting posture, with 60% of your weight on your rear foot (Fig. 81).

81

82

83

THE TWELVE STYLES

1. **DRAGON STYLE** (*Lung hsing*)

The DRAGON STYLE is a vigorous series of movements using vertical action from down to up and hardy leaps into a low, crouching form of the SPLITTING FIST.

From a left *san-t'i* (Fig. 81), shift your weight to your right leg and pull your hands back in fists as if pulling down on a rope. Bringing them across your waist toward the diagonal right rear, simultaneously retract your left foot and suspend it at your right ankle (Fig. 82). Continue by DRILLING your left fist upward to your head and your right fist upward to your left elbow. You are now facing sideways to the beginning posture (Fig. 83).

84   85   86

87   88   89

Next, turn your right fist over, opening it downward into a palm and SPLITTING it over your retracting left fist, which also opens and turns palm down. Simultaneously, lift your left foot and put it down toed-out in a scissor-step (Figs. 84, 85). You are now aligned to the right diagonal forward, your left hand at your right elbow. A triangle is formed by your right knee behind your left calf—but be careful not to bend your knees too much at first.

Now pull your hands back as you turn leftward (Fig. 86). DRILL your fists upward, and as they approach your middle begin to leap upward, carrying your arms high and forward, your right fist leading (Fig. 87). With your body in mid-air, open and extend your left hand,

90   91   92

93   94   95

turn it over, and SPLIT it out over your retracting right hand, which has also turned over, palm down. Simultaneously, alternate your right leg ahead of your left and land solidly in a scissor-step, toward the left diagonal (Figs. 88, 89).

Pulling your arms back and turning slightly rightward (Fig. 90), DRILL your hands upward, your left leading (Fig. 91), and leap up (Fig. 92), changing the lead leg in mid-air and landing solidly in a scissor-step, facing diagonally to the right, your right arm out (Fig. 93).

Pulling your arms back to your middle and turning slightly leftward (Fig. 94), shift your weight back to your right foot and move your left foot a half-step forward (Fig. 95). As your left foot drops, DRILL your

96   97   98

99   100   101

right fist upward, preparing to punch, and begin to swing your right leg forward (Fig. 96). Now, leap off your left foot, propelling your body directly forward, executing a right DRILLING punch and right stamping kick (Fig. 97).

Landing heel first on your toed-out left foot (Fig. 98), let your right leg drop forward and down into scissor-step (Fig. 99), turn your left hand over and SPLIT it over the retracting right hand as before, your body now oriented straight ahead (Fig. 100).

Shift your weight back to your left foot and take a half-step forward with your right foot. Clench your left hand into a fist and extend it slightly while clenching your right hand into a fist, palm up, at your hip. Simultaneously, suspend your left foot at your right ankle (Fig. 101).

102   103   104

105   106   107

Taking a full step forward with your left foot, do a right CRUSHING FIST while pulling your left fist back to your hip and follow-stepping with your right foot (Fig. 102). Turning back rightward, toe-in your left foot, and bring your fists, palms up, back to your hips (Fig. 103). Next, toe-out your right foot as you do a ''snake'' move with your right palm above it (Fig. 104), and, clenching your right palm into a fist, DRILL as your turn your knee out and wedge kick with your right foot (Fig. 105). Now put your right foot down toed-out, open both hands (Fig. 106), and, as you do a SPLITTING FIST with your left palm over your right straight ahead, lower your body by bending both knees into a scissor-step (Fig. 107).

Finally, bring the style to a close by taking a step to the right rear with the right foot and dropping your left arm on top of your right

108   109   110

111   112   113

(Fig. 108). Continue by lowering both arms (Fig. 109), and move your left foot to your right foot such that the heels touch. As you stand, raise your arms outward to shoulder level (Fig. 110) and bring them upward over your head as you turn your waist rightward (Fig. 111). Then, bending your knees together, press your hands down to your groin (Fig. 112). Lastly, stand up, facing diagonally to the right, taking your hands to your sides and raising your head slightly, your eyes up (Fig. 113). The ancients said that when you rest you should look up, which is good for health. This conventional close is done after each ANIMAL STYLE by bringing the right foot to the right rear and proceeding as outlined above. Once you have mastered the DRAGON STYLE starting from the left *san-t'i* position, do it from the right *san-t'i* position, reversing the directions above.

114   115   116

117   118   119

2. TIGER STYLE *(Hu hsing)*

The TIGER STYLE is done energetically, featuring an initial pull followed by a push.

From a left *san-t'i* (Fig. 114), move your right foot diagonally to the right (Fig. 115) as you pull your hands down in fists and turn your waist slightly rightward (Fig. 116). Suspend your left foot at your right ankle, your hands continuing in one motion from the pull and circling upward, palms down, to eyebrow level (Fig. 117). Turn leftward, hands dropping at eyebrow level, and step diagonally to the left with the left foot while extending your arms, the left slightly ahead of the right, with the "tiger's mouths" well open (Fig. 118). As you shift most of your weight back to your right foot, lower your hands slightly (Fig. 119).

THE TWELVE ANIMAL STYLES · **65**

120   121   122

123   124   125

Next, move your left foot a half-step forward diagonally to the left as your pull your hands down in fists to your left hip, and suspend your right foot at your left ankle (Fig. 120). Now raise your open hands, palm down, circularly upward to eyebrow level (Fig. 121) and turn your waist to face diagonally to the right (Fig. 122). Then take a step with the right foot diagonally to the right (Fig. 123), pressing your palms down, the right held slightly ahead of the left, stopping at chest level (Fig. 124).

To turn to go the other way, shift the weight onto your left foot and toe-in your right foot (Fig. 125). Next, shift the weight to your right foot and toe-out your left foot, turning your waist and swinging your arms leftward (Fig. 126). Take a step with your right foot diagonally to the right as you pull your fists to your right hip, and suspend your left

126   127   128

129   130   131

foot at your right ankle (Figs. 127, 128). Open your fists and raise your hands to eyebrow level (Fig. 129). Turn your waist to face diagonally to the left (Fig. 130), and step in that direction with your left foot, pressing your hands down to chest level, the left hand leading (Fig. 131). The press is done lightly, in contrast to the TIGER STYLE as taught in some other schools of Hsing-i, in which it is performed more powerfully. Practice the TIGER STYLE by alternating sides, zig-zagging from one diagonal to the other. The simple turn done with your right foot ahead, followed by one repetition of the form, is conventional for most of the ANIMAL STYLES. After one repetition in the new direction, ending with your left foot forward, step back with your right foot and do the closing as described at the end of the DRAGON STYLE (Figs. 108–13).

MONKEY

START - FINISH

1.

3.

N
W ● E
S

2.

4.

5.

132.   Directions in MONKEY STYLE   133

3.   MONKEY STYLE   (*Hou hsing*)

The MONKEY STYLE features retreating squats and advancing jumps to the four corners (Fig. 132).

Starting in a left *san-t'i* facing north (Fig. 133), circling out and down, retract your hands into fists, palms up, to your hips (Fig. 134), shift your weight onto your left foot, and step laterally to the right with your right foot as you do a right DRILLING FIST (Fig. 135). Without changing your fists, shift your weight onto the ball of your right foot and pivot on it until you face the northwest (NW) corner (Figs. 136, 137). This posture is fairly long, with your right foot holding at least 60% of your weight. As you move your right foot a long step backward, shoot your left palm out over your retracting right palm (Figs. 138, 139), and squat, toeing-in your left foot. Extend your left palm and hold your right palm under your left elbow (Fig. 140).

Now, toe-out your left foot, rise, and step toward the NW with your right foot as your right palm starts to spear over your retracting left palm (Figs. 141, 142). Continuing, hop off your right foot, following

134   135   136

137   138   139

140   141   142

143   144   145

146   147

through with your right palm, shooting forward and high (Figs. 143, 144). Your retracting left palm protects at your right elbow or under your chin, and your left knee is lifted high (Fig. 145). Next, lower your left foot and your arms to a left *san-t'i* facing NW (Figs. 146, 147).

Now, move your right foot laterally to the right as you use right DRILLING FIST (Figs. 148, 149), and pivot on the ball of your right foot until you face the southwest (SW) corner (Figs. 150, 151). Take a

148

149

150

151

152   153   154

full step backward with your right foot as before (Figs. 152, 153), squat, and toe-in your left foot slightly, extending your left palm as you retract your right palm under your left elbow (Fig. 154). Toeing out your left foot, step further to the SW with your right foot (Figs. 141, 142; although the photos of the sequence end here, we will refer to the previous photos illustrating the same position). Hopping on your right foot as before, spear your right palm over your retracting left palm (Figs. 143–45). Then, as you put your left foot down, extend your left arm and retract your right hand, moving into a left *san-t'i* position (Figs. 146, 147).

Using the photos for the previous two corners, go to the northeast (NE) corner, repeating the movement to *san-t'i*. Then repeat the movement to the southeast (SE) corner, ending in *san-t'i*.

To end, do the same sequence, going directly up the center. From *san-t'i* facing SE, step laterally to the right with your right foot and put it down opposite your left foot, doing a right DRILLING FIST. Bring your weight to your right foot and pivot as before (Figs. 136, 137) so that you face the front center in a right forward stance, your hands staying fixed as before. Now step back and squat on your right leg. Next, hop forward on your right foot while spearing with your right hand. Then lower your left foot and your hands into a left *san-t'i* position. Finally, step back with your right foot and do the conventional close.

For balance, after mastering the MONKEY STYLE from this side, begin with the right *san-t'i* position and do it from the other side doing the four corners in the sequence NE, SE, NW, and SW.

155

156

157

4. HORSE STYLE (*Ma hsing*)

The HORSE STYLE is a speedy and powerful posture in which the fists, palms down, strike together as you move forward in a zig-zag path.

From a left *san-t'i* (Fig. 155), as you step forward diagonally to the right with your right foot, change both hands into palm-up fists and bring them together, forearms close, swinging them straight down in front of your *tan-t'ien*. Simultaneously, suspend your left foot at your right ankle (Fig. 156).

Continue swinging your arms out laterally, fists on a line with your lower ribs (Fig. 157). Pause, then turn your arms over from the elbows, until your fists, palms down, line up with your shoulders. Hang your elbows and hold your right fist near your left elbow. Turning your waist leftward, step ahead diagonally to the left with your left

158   159   160

161   162

foot and punch forward with both "flat" fists, your left fist slightly ahead (Fig. 158). Finally, bring your right foot forward in a follow-step and shift 60% of your weight back onto it (Fig. 159). Use your waist: your navel should point directly ahead on the short steps and 45° on the long steps.

Continuing, step forward diagonally to the left with your left foot (Fig. 160) and suspend your right foot at your left ankle while swinging your arms down and out (Figs. 161, 162). Now, turn the waist, step diagonally to the right with your right foot, and circle your "flat" fists up and forward, your right held slightly ahead (Fig. 163). Follow-step with your left foot, shifting 60% of your weight back to it (Fig. 164).

163

164

Continue the alternate zig-zag step for four repetitions until your right leg is ahead. Turn back leftward and shift your weight to your left foot as you toe-in your right foot. Continue by shifting your weight back and toe-out your left foot. Next, step ahead diagonally to the right with your right foot and change both hands to palm-up fists and bring them together, forearms close, swinging them straight down in front of your *tan-t'ien*. Simultaneously, suspend your left foot at your right ankle (refer back to Fig. 156). Turn your arms over as before, turn your waist, and step ahead diagonally to the left with your left foot as you punch with both "flat" fists, your left slightly ahead (refer back to Figs. 157–159). Finally, step back a short step with your right foot and do the conventional close.

165 166

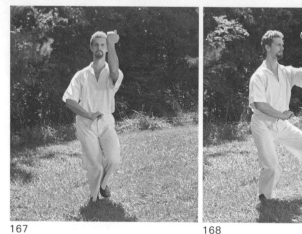

167 168

5. WATER STRIDER STYLE (*T'ou hsing*)

The WATER STRIDER STYLE resembles the "Cloud Hands" (*Yun shou*) posture of T'ai-chi and emphasizes the flexibility of the waist.   From a left *san-t'i* (Fig. 165), retract your left foot and suspend it at your right ankle while circling your left hand down counterclockwise as you turn your waist rightward (Fig. 166), stopping your left fist in front of your eyes (Fig. 167). Hold your right fist, palm down, at your navel. You are now facing sideways from the *san-t'i* position. Step ahead diagonally to the left with your left foot and roll your waist leftward, carrying your left arm, held at a right angle, across your body (Fig. 168).

Continue turning your waist and left fist, palm in, leftward, shifting your weight to your left foot. As the hand passes the front, turn it out-

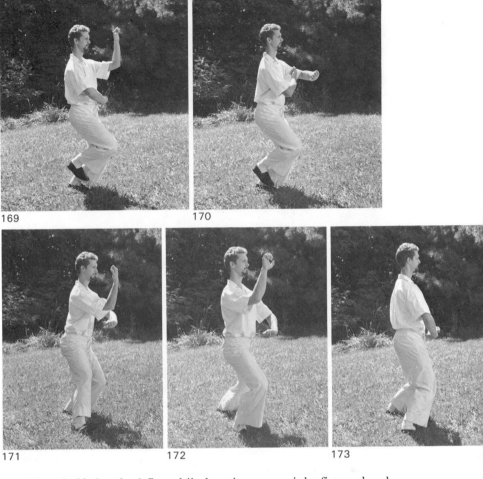

169   170

171   172   173

ward in a half-clenched fist while keeping your right fist, palm down, at your *tan-t'ien*, and suspend your right foot at your left ankle (Fig. 169).

Alternate sides by turning your waist rightward as you take your right fist inside your extended left arm in a clockwise circle (Fig. 170), at the same time stepping ahead diagonally to the right with your right foot (Fig. 171). Continue rolling your waist rightward until your right half-clenched fist is in front of your eyes, your left fist is at your *tan-t'ien*, and your body is turned past the center to the right (Fig. 172).

Continue the alternating zig-zag step for four repetitions until your right leg is ahead, when you can turn around. Toe-in your right foot as you circle your right fist to your *tan-t'ien*, next to your left fist (Fig. 173). Next, withdraw your left foot and suspend it at your right ankle as you screw your left fist up ahead of your body at eyebrow level (Fig. 174). Turning leftward, move your left foot diagonally to the left (Fig.

174

175   176

175), and, as you shift your weight to your left foot, turn your left forearm outward in deflection as your right fist, palm down, stays at your *tan-t'ien*, and suspend your right foot at your left ankle (Fig. 176). Finally, step back with your right foot and do the conventional close.

177 178 179

180 181

6. COCK STYLE (*Chi hsing*)

The COCK STYLE stresses strong legs and adroit arms.

From a left *san-t'i* (Fig. 177), shift more of your weight back to your right foot and let your left heel come off the ground as you relax your arms, raising your right hand to near your left elbow, and drooping the fingers of both hands (Fig. 178). Take a half-step directly forward with your left foot (Fig. 179), and, as you shift your weight onto it, move your right palm beneath your left forearm up and forward, suspending your right foot at your left ankle (Figs. 180, 181). Pause, drooping your hands slightly.

THE TWELVE ANIMAL STYLES • 79

182

183

184

Then step forward with your right foot and move your left palm beneath your right forearm up and forward (Fig. 182), while suspending your left foot at your right ankle (Fig. 183). Pause.

Then raise your arms slightly (Fig. 184) and step forward with your left foot (Fig. 185), pressing down with both palms (Fig. 186). Follow-step with your right foot and do a left *san-t'i*.

Do four repetitions of the COCK STYLE, moving in a straight line. After the first repetition, it is not necessary to shift your weight back and droop your arms as shown in Figure 178. Simply shift your weight forward onto your left foot and repeat the movement as shown above (Fig. 186).

Turn around by pivoting on your heels 180° rightward so that you face the opposite direction in the right *san-t'i* position. Then do the

185

186

COCK STYLE four times in the other direction by reversing the instructions above. As a standard form, however, starting from the left *san-t'i* position, do a series of four repetitions and then, with your left foot forward, turn around 180° into the right *san-t'i* position and do one repetition. Finally, move your leading right foot backward and do the conventional close. Alternatively, you may practice as many repetitions as you have room to do in each direction.

187   188

189   190

7. FALCON STYLE (*Yao hsing*)

The FALCON STYLE is sharp and emphasizes the fist used with both a contracted and an opened body.

From the left *san-t'i* position (Fig. 187), withdraw and sink, emptying your left foot. Change your hands into fists, moving your right fist, palm up, to your right hip and lowering your left standing fist on a line with your left leg (Fig. 188).

Shift your weight to your left foot and move your right foot forward, pausing above your left ankle (Fig. 189). Now, as you stamp your right foot down, punch with a standing right fist over your left fist and suspend your left foot at your right ankle (Fig. 190).

As you step forward with your left foot, arc both arms outward and

191

192

193

down, the right inside the left (Figs. 191, 192). Shift your weight to your left foot as you drop your fists, your right slightly higher than your left. Your left fist should align with your left ear; your right fist, with your eyebrows. Then look at your right hand and shift your weight so that you are 60% rear-weighted (Fig. 193).

After repeating the FALCON STYLE several times on one side, turn around by toeing in your left leading foot and toeing out your rear foot and going in the other direction, using your left fist and stamping with your left foot. As a standard form, however, starting from the left *san-t'i* position, do a series with your right fist and foot, turn around and do one with your left fist and foot, and finish by moving the leading right foot backward past the left and doing the conventional close.

194 195

196 197 198

8. SWALLOW STYLE (*Yen hsing*)

The SWALLOW STYLE is an invigorating blend of soaring and squatting.

From a left *san-t'i* (Fig. 194), step forward with your right foot, toed-out, depressing forward and down with your right hand as you press with your left hand under your right elbow (Fig. 195). Shift all of your weight onto your right foot and lift your left leg, holding the foot before the right knee with toes pointing down, as you begin a large clockwise circle with your right drooping hand (Fig. 196). Turn your waist rightward, your right hand at eyebrow level (Fig. 197), and put your left foot down ahead, shifting 40% of your weight onto it. You should now be turned toward the right and looking at your right index finger (Fig. 198).

199   200

201   202

As you shift most of your weight to your left foot, your right hand continues circling around and down past the right side of your body (Fig. 199), and, as your weight goes fully onto your left leg, raise your right hand as before, but this time with your right foot held suspended before your left knee (Fig. 200).

Turn your waist rightward and move your right hand, palm out, in another circle, your left hand accompanying it by pivoting from the left elbow (Fig. 201). When your hands are at the highest point, jump off your left foot and land on your right foot as you extend your right hand backward from its circle, changing it into a "pecking hand" (similar to that used in the "Single Whip" [*tan-pien*] posture of T'ai-chi). Hold your left hand near your right elbow and left knee high, the left foot held before the right knee with toes pointing down (Fig. 202).

203   204   205

206   207

208   209   210

Now extend your left foot to the front, dropping most of your weight onto your right leg, sinking into a low squat. Stretch your left hand, palm down, down along your left leg to your ankle. Simultaneously, turn your right "pecking hand" over toward the rear, so that the fingers point up (Fig. 203).

Rise and shift your weight to your left leg, bringing your right hand, palm up, to your right hip while extending your left hand slightly, palm down (Fig. 204). Now step forward with your right foot and begin to raise your right hand, palm up (Fig. 205). Move your right hand, stabbing forward and upward to shoulder level as your weight shifts fully to your right leg, your left foot suspended at your right ankle. Simultaneously, slap your right forearm with your left palm (Fig. 206).

Next, change your open hands into fists (Fig. 207), step forward with your left foot, and punch directly ahead with a left CRUSHING FIST. At the same time, retract your right fist, palm up, to your right hip and follow-step with your right foot (Fig. 208).

Toe-out your left foot, raise your left hand, palm down (Fig. 209), and take a full step forward with your right foot while doing a right DRILLING FIST over your depressing left hand. Change your left open hand into a palm-down fist at your right elbow as you follow-step with your left foot. Your weight is now 60% backloaded (Fig. 210).

After performing one SWALLOW STYLE movement, with your right foot ahead in the DRILLING FIST, turn leftward to face the other direction by toeing-in your right foot and toeing-out your left foot, keeping your hands in the DRILLING FIST position. Then drop your hands and step back with your right foot in the conventional close.

For free practice, if there is room enough, you may simply step forward with your left foot past the DRILLING FIST into the left *san-t'i* position and do another SWALLOW STYLE form, repeating the directions above. If there is insufficient room, turn around after each repetition and do it going in the opposite direction. Because of its complexity, do the SWALLOW STYLE only from a left *san-t'i* until you master it, and then try it from a right *san-t'i,* reversing the directions given above.

THE TWELVE ANIMAL STYLES • **87**

211

212

213

9. SNAKE STYLE (*She hsing*)

The SNAKE STYLE stresses elasticity and palms shooting up from a crouching posture.

From the left *san-t'i* position (Fig. 211), retract your left foot and suspend it at your right ankle. Pivoting at the left elbow, move the forearm in a small arc and pierce down the center of your body. Turn your left palm so that it faces your left knee and raise your right palm so that it protects your left shoulder (Fig. 212).

Turn your left hand over so that the palm faces out (Fig. 213), and step directly forward with your left foot (Fig. 214). As your right foot follow-steps, your forward momentum carries your left hand upward, striking with the wrist-top, while your right hand retracts to your right

214

215

216

hip (Fig. 215). Sink slightly, shifting your weight back onto your right leg, and snap your left hand upward from the wrist. You now hold your right hand, palm down, at your right hip (Fig. 216).

Alternate sides by taking a half-step with your left foot, toed out, and slicing your right hand down the center of your body, reversing the directions above. Do four repetitions. With your right foot and hand forward, toe-in your right foot and turn back leftward to the other direction with your left foot in the left *san-t'i* position. Drop back as shown in Figure 212, and do one repetition of the SNAKE STYLE form, ending with your left foot forward, as shown in Figure 216. Lastly, step back with your right foot and do the conventional close.

THE TWELVE ANIMAL STYLES · **89**

217   218

219   220

10.   T'AI STYLE   (*T'ai hsing*)

The T'AI (a mythical bird) STYLE briskly zig-zags forward while generating power by an initial circling of the arms upward, in contrast to the HORSE STYLE'S initial circling downward.

From a left *san-t'i* (Fig. 217), take a step forward diagonally to the right with your right foot (Fig. 218) and raise your right arm under your left, both forearms going overhead as your left foot follows to suspend at your right ankle (Fig. 219). Pull your arms apart, completing the circle, stopping your fists, palms up, at your hips (Fig. 220). Turn your waist leftward and step forward diagonally to the left with your left foot (Fig. 221), and punch down with your right fist, palm down, over your extended palm-down left fist. Follow-step and shift your weight back to your rear foot (Fig. 222).

90 · CHAPTER 5

221

222

To alternate sides, take a half-step with your left foot further along the left diagonal, suspending your right foot at your left ankle, raise your arms, left under right, and circle out and down, stopping at your hips, palms up. Then turn your waist rightward and step with your right foot to the diagonal as you punch with your left fist, palm down, over your right fist.

After four repetitions on this zig-zag path, you end with your right foot forward and your body facing diagonally to the right. To turn back leftward to the other direction, toe-in your right foot, toe-out your left foot, and step to the right front with your right foot, circling your arms, and suspend your left foot at your right ankle. Pause and then take a step directly forward with your left foot and punch with right "flat" fist over your left arm, follow-step with your right foot, and shift 60% of your weight back onto it. Finally, step further back with your right foot and do the conventional close.

223

224

225

11. & 12. COMBINED EAGLE-AND-BEAR STYLE
(*Ying-Hsiung hsing*)

The COMBINED EAGLE-AND-BEAR STYLE integrates the properties of yin and yang, the straight and the oblique, and the up and the down; it also features the SPLITTING FIST done diagonally.

From a left *san-t'i* (Fig. 223), copy the first part of the DRAGON STYLE: Shift your weight to your right leg and pull your hands back in fists as if pulling on a rope. Bringing them across your waist toward the right hip. Simultaneously, retract your left foot and suspend it at your right ankle (Fig. 224). DRILL your left fist upward to your head, and your right fist upward at your left elbow. You are now in a position sideways to the beginning posture (Fig. 225).

Next, turn your right fist over, opening it palm downward, and

226

227

228

SPLIT it over your retracting left hand, which opens and turns palm-down. Simultaneously, lift your left foot and put it down, toed-out, in a scissor-step (Fig. 226). You are now aligned to the right diagonal forward, your left hand at your right elbow. Keep the triangle formed by your right knee behind your left calf—but be careful not to bend your knees too much at first.

Take a half-step with your left foot diagonally across to the right and pull your hands back into palm-up fists at your left hip (Fig. 227). As you shift your weight onto your left foot, DRILL your right fist upward and high diagonally to the left, your left fist following your right elbow. Simultaneously, suspend your right foot at your left ankle (Fig. 228).

Now step further diagonally to the right with your right foot as you

229

230

231

232

233

234

235

236

237

238

open your left hand and press it forward, SPLITTING over your right palm (Fig. 229). As your right foot goes down, stop your left palm at eye level and your right palm at your *tan-t'ien*. Follow-step with your left foot (Fig. 230).

Alternate sides by stepping with your right foot diagonally across to the left as you pull your hands to your right hip (Fig. 231). Then, suspending your left foot at your right ankle, DRILL your left fist diagonally to the right (Fig. 232). Now step further diagonally to the left with your left foot, SPLITTING your right palm over your left palm (Figs. 233, 234).

Next, do a third repetition, pulling your hands leftward as you step rightward with your left foot (Fig. 235), suspending your right foot and DRILLING your right fist (Fig. 236). Finish off by stepping out with your right foot while SPLITTING your left palm over your right palm and follow-stepping with your left foot (Figs. 237, 238).

Turn and do one repetition in the other direction to complete the

239

240

241

242

form. To turn around, toe-in your right foot and toe-out your left foot (Fig. 239), and step diagonally toward the right with your left foot as you retract your fists to your left hip (Fig. 240). Now DRILL with your right fist diagonally to the the left and suspend your right foot as before (Fig. 241). Then, open your left fist and SPLIT it over your retracting right hand as you put your right foot down. As before, your left palm stops at eyebrow level and your right palm at the *tan-t'ien* (Fig. 242). Finally, step backward with your right foot and do a conventional close.

6
Conclusion

The popularity of Hsing-i in China was greatly increased through the skill and the books of the famous Sun Lu-t'ang, whose *Ch'uan-i Shu Cheng* [The Real Explanation of Boxing (1929)] was written to present the true aspects of the art. We have used some of the information contained in his book in introducing the art and the Hsing-i masters. It is only natural, therefore, that we end this presentation with his own words.

> The Tao permeates the universe and is the origin of both yin and yang. In boxing, the Tao is symbolized by the internal arts of Hsing-i, Pa-kua, and T'ai-chi. Although these three arts are different, they are based upon the same principle: everything begins, is, and ends in emptiness. One's original energy (*yuan ch'i*) must be maintained. This is the power that keeps the sky blue and that makes the earth calm and also makes for achievement in man. . . . Confucius said: "From the greatest sincerity comes the greatest achievement."

Diligent practice in the internal arts is a discipline, a system of self-control over conduct. The Latin root of the word discipline means both "rigor" and "education"—a leading forth of your true self. Although Chinese, the three internal martial arts of Hsing-i, Pa-kua, and T'ai-chi are excellent expressions of what the ancient Greeks called *aretē*—a noble ideal that Plato called "the holistic striving for excellence in terms of beauty, strength, and wisdom.'' As in *aretē*, excellence in the internal arts is only possible while one is striving. Those who think that they have attained excellence have already lost it, bypassing *aidos* (modesty) for hubris, or overbearing pride. Therefore, in order to best perfect your Hsing-i skills, always work hard and remain humble.

Index

Hopei, 18
HORSE STYLE, 57, 73–75
Hou hsing, 68–72
hsin, 27
Hsing-i: basic posture of, 30, see also *san-t'i*; becomes a part of your life, 14; as boxing with the mind, 19; and Buddhist/Taoist practices, 16, 21; as cooperative, 16; and dedication, 15; history of, 17–18; as an internal art, 13, 14; and muscles/ligaments, 19; as natural as a baby's movements, 32; and single/double weighting, 20–21; as training the mind even more than it does the body, 15; as unique, 14; used only in the greatest extremity, 14
hsing-i ch'uan, 13
hsu, 14
Hu hsing, 65–67
Hu k'ou, 26–27
hubris, 98

INFINITY POSTURE, 33, 34, 50, 51, 55
inguinal crease, 34
internal fighting systems, as different from the Shaolin, 13n
intrinsic energy, 14, 19

Japanese martial arts, 15

Kuo Yun-shen, 14–15, 18, 19, 21, 36–37

Li Cheng, 18

Li Neng-jan, 18
Li Ts'un-i, 18
linked form, 51–55
Lung hsing, 59–64

Ma hsing, 73–75
Ma Hsueh-li, 18
Mallory, 14
method of transforming the self, 14
MONKEY STYLE, 57, 68–72
muscular strength, 13n
mysterious energy, 22

Nanking, 15
Nine Words, 26–28

original *ch'i,* 20, 97
original emptiness, 14
original state, 14
original state of emptiness, 14
orthodox Hsing-i, 18, 32
overturning, 28

pact, requiring students of Hsing-i and Pa-kua to cross train, 15
Pa-kua, 13, 14, 15, 21, 28, 97
P'ao ch'uan, 32, 45–46
"pecking hand," 85, 87
Peng ch'uan, 32, 40–41
physiological and esoteric principles, 21
P'i ch'uan, 32, 36–39
Plato, 97–98
POUNDING FIST, 32, 45–46, 51, 53
pre-birth energy, 22

Other Titles in the Tuttle Library of Martial Arts

AIKIDO AND THE DYNAMIC SPHERE
by Adele Westbrook and Oscar Ratti

Aikido is a Japanese method of self-defense that can be used against any form of attack and that is also a way of harmonizing all of one's vital powers into an integrated, energy-filled whole.

BLACK BELT KARATE *by Jordan Roth*

A no-frills, no-holds barred handbook on the fundamentals of modern karate. Over 800 techniques and exercises and more than 1,850 photographs reveal the speed and power inherent in properly taught karate.

THE ESSENCE OF OKINAWAN KARATE-DO
by Shoshin Nagamine

"Nagamine's book will awaken in all who read it a new understanding of the Okinawan open-handed martial art."

—Gordon Warner
Kendo 7th dan, renshi

THE HAND IS MY SWORD: A KARATE HANDBOOK *by Robert A. Trias*

The history, the fundamentals, and the basic techniques and katas are brought to life by over 600 illustrations in this book, which teaches that to master others one must first master oneself.

SECRETS OF THE SAMURAI *by Oscar Ratti and Adele Westbrook*

A definitive study of the martial arts of feudal Japan, illustrating the techniques, weapons, strategies, and principles of combat that made the Japanese samurai a terrible foe.

SECRETS OF SHAOLIN TEMPLE BOXING *edited by Robert W. Smith*

Abundantly and attractively illustrated, this book presents the essence of Shaolin in three sections— its history, its fundamentals, and its techniques— gleaned from a rare Chinese text.

SHAOLIN: AN INTRODUCTION TO LOHAN FIGHTING TECHNIQUES *by P'ng Chye Khim and Donn F. Draeger*

A clearly written manual giving detailed explanations of the special elements of South China's Lohan style of Shaolin.

T'AI-CHI: THE "SUPREME ULTIMATE" EXERCISE *by Cheng Man-ch'ing and Robert W. Smith*

Written by one of the leading Yang-style experts, who studied directly under the legendary Yang Cheng-fu (d. 1935), this book illustrates Cheng's famous short form and includes a translation of the *T'ai-chi Ch'uan Classics*.

THIS IS KENDO *by Junzo Sasamori and Gordon Warner*

The first book in English to describe the origin and history of kendo, its basic principles and techniques.

Robert W. Smith, is famous for his pioneering work in introducing the Chinese martial arts to the West; many of his texts are classics in the field. **Allen Pittman,** Smith's senior student, collaborated on this book after several years of full-time study and research in Taiwan.